Eat the
F*cking Pizza!

Simplifying healthy to help you
live with Rockin' Vitality

MARY SCHRANK

Self Published - Sarasota, Florida
2023

DEDICATION PAGE

This book is dedicated to the health and wellness industry that creates endless contradictions and over-complicates everything, including how to toast toast. Without your confusion and quest to push perfection, this book wouldn't be necessary, so I 'preciate ya.

CONTENTS

FOREWORD

Almost 2 years ago, I had broken my ankle, was 45 pounds heavier, and was completely miserable. I had lost my true self physically, emotionally, and mentally. I was an empty nester as my daughter was away at college, and I was still in the process of putting myself back together after ending an abusive relationship. I was truly in an awful place!

Until, one day, I was scrolling on TikTok for way too long, you know, as one does, lol. And I found Mary! The rest is history…

If someone had told me on that day when I felt like total crap about myself that I would find Mary, this amazing program, and by August of 2023 I'd feel this good, I would have laughed at them! Well, here I am feeling better than I've ever felt, not just because I lost 40 pounds and look better, but because I feel whole again in ALL aspects of my life!

This program, along with Mary's energy and inspiration, has truly saved my life and given me such purpose. At 55 years old I feel better physically, emotionally, and mentally than I did in my 20's. I'm so proud of myself, and so blessed to be able to be a part of such an amazing program that is sustainable for life! I thank God every day for bringing Mary into my life at just the right time. Everything really does happen for a reason!

Mary, thank you for your support, guidance, and holding me accountable, but most of all… Thank you for your friendship and belief in me that I could do this for myself!

Sheri K Stella

PROLOGUE

Serious Disclaimer: I am going to speak throughout this book about eating "stupid foods" in moderation. HOWEVER, it should go without saying, but I'm gonna say it anyway, that if you have a medical condition in which certain foods are a BIG NO NO, you should avoid those foods altogether.

Let me begin by saying...

If you are looking for a new "diet," put this book down.

If you are looking for a magic pill or shake or sorcery on a spoon, put this book down.

If you are looking for new workout moves, put this book down.

If you are looking for a book full of healthy recipes, put this book down.

If you are looking for a seemingly perfect person to teach you "healthy perfect", put this book down.

HOWEVER...

If you are looking for a SIMPLE approach to healthy, you found it here!

If you are looking for a FUN approach to healthy, you found it here!

If you are looking for an AFFORDABLE approach to healthy, you found it here!

If you are looking for a healthy lifestyle that is truly SUSTAINABLE FOREVER, you found it here!

If you are looking for an author with a sense of humor to keep you laughing, smiling, engaged, and ON FIRE for life again, yep, say it with me...you found it here!

Listen, I haven't always been this healthy. I thought choosing the blueberry Pop-tart over the chocolate for breakfast was a great start to the day. I was skinny as a rail growing up… Turn me sideways, and I was gone, but that's not because I was exposed to or living a healthy lifestyle. Don't get me wrong, my upbringing and parents were fantastic, but we grew up on Mrs. Paul's fish sticks and mac and cheese, not chicken and broccoli. So you don't know what you don't know.

I headed off to college after high school and managed to blow by the "Freshman 15", all thanks to excessive alcohol, drugs, 2am Taco Bell, and Lucky Charms after every dining hall meal. I hit the checkered flag with a whopping 30-pound weight gain by Christmas break!

I went on to become a proud, degreed TSU graduate and a non-licensed Chronic Yo-Yo'er. I spent the next 15 years beating my head against the wall, trying to find consistency with healthy habits. I'd do good for about three months, then fu…dge! I'd fall off the wagon. Three months later, I'd get sick and tired of being sick and tired and get back on the wagon again…only to fall right back off three months later… and on and on and on this cycle of madness went.

I would ask everyone I knew who seemed to have it all figured out how they were able to stay so consistent, why weren't they falling off the wagon like I was every three months?! They all answered me the same way, "You just have to exercise and eat healthy." Well, no shit Sherlock, I understand the WHAT…I need to know the HOW. So, as embarrassed as I am to admit this, I tried every fad diet, every fad program, every personal trainer, and every horribly dangerous diet pill out there. I spent so much money, even risked my life, and saw ZERO RESULTS.

Then, in July of 2008, my Personal Trainer at the gym, LeeAnn, stopped me in the middle of my training session to tell me about a home-based full wellness system that was working so well for her husband. She strongly encouraged me to try it, even while knowing that she'd lose me as a client. She knew I needed a full wellness system, not just the great workouts that she could offer. We simply cannot out-workout a poor diet, and I was living proof of that.

I strongly resisted, but agreed to try it for 30 days. Then, I watched weeks turn into months, which turned into years of consistency with my healthy habits. I couldn't believe it…I had finally found the solution to my problem! I haven't been back to the gym for regular workouts since that day.

So, what was the game-changing difference? Two things: ACCOUNTABILITY and a nutrition plan that allows for treats (aka life) in moderation, which means it is truly SUSTAINABLE FOR LIFE.

It doesn't matter if we know what to do; we ALL need someone who NOTICES and CARES when we're not showing up and respectfully taps us on the shoulder to keep us in the game.

In 2012, after 4 solid years of consistency with my healthy habits, I decided to pay this amazing gift forward and start my online Health & Wellness business. I built it part-time for three years while still working my full-time corporate job. Then, in 2015, I was blessed to say goodbye to Corporate America and now spend my days helping you live your best life like I am.

At the time of writing this book I am 52 years old and am proud to say that I am happier and healthier than I've ever been in my entire life! My goal, my purpose, my calling from God is to help you say the same. He's using me in a very powerful way, and I pray that my words in this book, while sometimes full of quirkiness, humor, and an occasional Fbomb, will impact your life in a very profound way.

Are you ready to breathe easier, relax your shoulders, and put a HUGE SMILE on your face as I teach you step-by-step how to SIMPLIFY HEALTHY in a way you may have never heard before?

LET'S GOOOOOOOOOO!

YOUR MIND

GETTING HEALTHY BETWEEN THE EARS

We've got to work on the muscle BETWEEN THE EARS before we even begin to think about working on the glam muscles.

Our thoughts are super powerful!

Our **THOUGHTS** control our **FEELINGS**, which control our **ACTIONS**, which control the **OUTCOME** of our lives. So, our **THOUGHTS** truly control the **OUTCOME** of our lives.

The Wall Street Journal published a fantastic article on October 13, 2023, titled "The Power of Your Exercise Mindset" by Jenny Taitz, stating:

If exercise seems like a great idea, but you can never keep up a routine, it's worth considering your exercise "mindset"—defined by psychologists as core assumptions that shape our behavior and reality. While it's long been known that mindsets can make a big difference in academic performance and navigating stress, evidence is mounting that targeting some of our most ingrained, habitual beliefs and replacing them with more adaptive ones can rev up our ability to keep ourselves healthy. "Whether they're true or false, mindsets have an impact," says Dr. Alia Crum, who runs the Stanford Mind & Body Lab. "They change what we pay attention to, what we're motivated to do, how we feel emotionally about what we're doing, and what we decide to prioritize."

Basically, Dr. Crum's statement can be summed up in one of my favorite quotes, *"Whether you think you can, or you think you can't—you're right."* - Henry Ford

So how do we get our **THOUGHTS** aligned with the **OUTCOME** we desire for our lives?

CREATE YOUR ROADMAP:

STEP 1.

Develop your WHY: your purpose and your reason. Define WHY you want to reach your wellness goals. And no, you can't answer "to be healthy." Duh, we all want to be healthy. Dig deeper… How will you FEEL when you reach your goals and are healthy? Maybe you want to feel more confident, have more energy, or be proud of yourself. Maybe, like me, it's to live without limitations in your life. Or maybe you just want to freakin' feel like that sexy beast that lives inside of you again…she's still there, Cheeka, waiting for you to find her.

STEP 2.

Start each day by reading or listening to 10 minutes of something positive. Feed your brain healthy fuel to build your armor and protect you from the negativity the day may bring your way…and you can trust and believe that someone or something will work hard to bring you down almost every single day.

You don't have to FIND or MAKE time for this important habit; you can ANCHOR it right to another.

I listen to an audiobook or podcast at 0:DARK:30 while I'm brushing my teeth and washing my face; I simply anchor this habit to something I already do daily.

Your book or audio can be spiritual, educational, or motivational…it doesn't matter the subject; however, it MUST be uplifting and positive to get your thoughts aligned with your goals and dreams.

STEP 3.

Surround yourself with people who lift you up versus drag you down. We become the average of the five people we spend the most time with. Who are your five?

We may not have control over all five; some in our five are close family, and they aren't ALL uplifting. However, not all five are, so be very selective with filling those other spots. This doesn't mean we have to cut people completely out of our lives who are negative, but I would highly encourage you to limit your time with them. I do. I love them and still see or talk to them on occasion, but not on the daily. I simply value my life too much to allow someone else to control it.

STEP 4.

Keep. It. Simple. Stupid. And yes, we're using the word STUPID because we're not 5, and I want to piss you off (anger can become positive fuel if we allow it). We must find SIMPLICITY. Overcomplication messes with our heads BIGTIME and usually causes us to quit before we've even gotten started. Society, media, and people everywhere will find 12 ways from Sunday to overcomplicate the simplest of things. Drives me nuts!

And the health and wellness industry, good gracious, it wins the GOLD…top of the podium, baby…for overcomplication!

So, how do you weed through all of this mess and create healthy habits that are simple? You find a full wellness system that allows for life in moderation, and you test your body to determine what works best for YOU. Not what works best for Trainer Troy, Fitness Fran, or Nutritionist Nancy.

Don't misunderstand what I'm saying; the experts bring us expert advice from reliable sources and test groups, and I encourage you to listen and learn. However, not everyone's body is the same, so the only way you can determine what will work best for YOU is to test their recommendations on YOUR own body.

STEP 5.

Ok, this last one might sting a little, but I'm not here to feed you sugar. I'm here to shoot straight, respectfully, and help you truly live at your highest potential.

STOP WISHIN & BITCHIN. KNOCK IT OFF! It's not too late, and you're not too old to start feeling your best.

Stop telling me and others that you "wish you [fill in the blank] like us." I know you are intending it as a compliment, but it just pisses me off. Why? Because I want you to stop WISHING for things that you can absolutely have and stop BITCHING about how you look and feel and rather DO SOMETHING ABOUT IT!

Those that you see and WISH you had what they have are not unicorns. They have simply adopted a handful of daily habits that have compounded over time to create the good things in their lives. You can do the exact same.

You give me your list of obstacles and I'll put you in touch with my clients working out from their knees or in their wheelchairs who are living their best lives.

"Your age isn't stopping you from living your best life, your excuses are." - Mel Robbins

BOTTOM LINE:

When your thoughts are positive, healthy, and simple, and the people you associate with are uplifting, this will lead you down a road to success.

Your **THOUGHTS** control your **FEELINGS**

Your **FEELINGS** control your **ACTIONS**.

Your **ACTIONS** control the **OUTCOME** of your life.

Therefore…

Your **THOUGHTS** control the **OUTCOME** of your life!

MINDSET SUCCESS STORY:

REGINA LIVELY
47 / Oklahoma / 50lb weight loss

When I began my healthier lifestyle a year and a half ago, what helped me get started was finding my WHY. What has kept me on the right track is working on my mindset daily. I started listening to short daily personal development videos and audiobooks while driving. Now, I also incorporate my personal development into my morning workouts, a practice called habit stacking. Each morning, either before or after my workout, I listen to a quick personal development video and share a snippet of it in my accountability group. Working on my mindset in this way has helped me change negative self-talk into positive self-talk. It has also helped me accept myself as I am today while knowing that each day, I will be a better version of myself than I was the day before.

2

YOUR HABITS

Everything we do circles back to our habits…both good and bad. If we dig back deep enough, the reason why we do the things we do is because, many times, they've simply become a habit. Let this make you smile ear to ear because habits, while not always easy to change and adopt, are 100% within our control, so you don't have to rely on anyone but yourself to create change.

Chapter 1 was on mindset for a reason because, as you learned, our **THOUGHTS** control our **FEELINGS**, which control our **ACTIONS** (aka our habits). So, you guessed it, to adopt new habits, we must first analyze our THOUGHTS about our current habits and the new habit(s) we are looking to adopt.

When we repeat a behavior frequently, our brains create neural pathways that make it easier for us to perform that behavior without conscious thought. This process is known as habit formation. Whether it's brushing our teeth, driving a car, or reaching for a snack when we're stressed, habits streamline our actions and free up mental bandwidth for more complex tasks.

SIDEBAR: That's the most nerdy scientific I'll get in this book, but we all passed BIO in HS, so I knew you could handle it.

Think for a minute about a poor habit you have…maybe it's smoking or drinking or watching too much TV, etc. Do you analyze your decision to do that thing every single time you do it? Or do you find yourself doing it at the same time every day, almost subconsciously, without even making an intentional choice to do it?

I'll bet the latter is true because it is for me too. We simply run our routines many times on autopilot like robots. But good news! If we can get robotic and run our poor habits on autopilot, guess what? We can run some good, healthy habits on autopilot just the same, allowing them to become intrinsic, almost as routine as brushing your teeth. Isn't that so refreshing to learn?

At the core of every habit (both good and bad habits) is a loop. The **HABIT LOOP** consists of three components: cue, routine, and reward.

CUE: This is the trigger that initiates the habit. It can be a specific time of day, a particular location, an emotional state, or even the presence of other people. Cues serve as the starting point for our habits, signaling our brain to enter autopilot mode.

ROUTINE: The routine is the behavior or action that follows the cue. It's the actual habit we want to either establish or break. This is where the brain conserves energy by simply going into autopilot and following a well-trodden path.

REWARD: The reward is the positive outcome or feeling we get from completing the routine. It reinforces the habit loop and encourages us to repeat the behavior in the future. Rewards can be physical, emotional, or psychological.

So, how do we INTENTIONALLY make better choices each day so our ROUTINES work FOR us and not against us? I've got some great tips to pass along to you. Some I learned from my amazing mentors, and some I made up myself.

Changing habits can be challenging but so rewarding. Whether you want to kick a bad habit or develop a positive one, the key lies in understanding and manipulating the habit loop.

Identify the CUE: Start by pinpointing the cue that triggers the habit you want to change. Is it stress, boredom, or a specific time of day? Knowing your cue will help you anticipate when the habit might be triggered.

Replace the ROUTINE: Once you've identified the cue, work on substituting the routine with a healthier alternative. For example, if stress triggers your habit of reaching for unhealthy snacks, try going for a short walk or practicing deep breathing instead.

REWARD Yourself: Make sure to reward yourself for completing the new routine. The reward should be satisfying enough to reinforce the positive behavior. Over time, your brain will associate the new routine with a positive outcome, making it more likely to stick.

CREATE YOUR ROADMAP:

STEP 1

Decide which habits you'd like to nix from your routine and which you'd like to adopt.

STEP 2

Take a close look at your very detailed daily calendar. Make an honest assessment of the time blocks, those that are your true priorities that must remain, things that are nice but not critical, things that could be shifted, and things that could be removed entirely.

STEP 3

Then begin planning/scheduling your new habits. Keep in mind that not all of them will require ADDITIONAL time; some can be anchored onto another habit. James Clear teaches about habit anchoring in his book Atomic Habits. You simply anchor a new habit onto a habit that's already intrinsic, one that's already a rock-solid fixture in your routine. For example, as I mentioned earlier, I anchor my daily personal development mindset work every single morning to brushing my teeth. I press play and listen to my audiobook/podcast/etc. while I'm brushing my teeth and washing my face.

STEP 4

Establishing an early morning routine/habit is a big challenge for many of us, BUT trust me, it's totally doable. I was the Snooze Button Queen over here; just ask My Paul. Now, my early morning routine/habit is so rock solid that my body alarm goes off at 0:DARK:30, even on the weekends. I'll cover more on this in the YOUR WORKOUTS Chapter, so stay tuned.

STEP 5

This one is a BIG ONE and one that has stopped me from falling off the wagon on many occasions. I call it MARY'S 3-DAY RULE: Never hit day 3 of poor choices. Miss a workout or two, no worries, no guilt, but NEVER miss 3 in a row! Have some stupid foods a day or two, no worries, no guilt...although your belly will be screaming at you...but NEVER eat stupid food for 3 days straight!

STEP 6

Last and most important, you MUST have an accountability partner. Someone who NOTICES and CARES when you aren't "showing up" and directly, yet respectfully, taps you on the shoulder to keep you on that wagon. I'm telling you that this has been the key to my consistency and the key for all of my clients who have been consistent with me for years.

BOTTOM LINE:

Habits are the building blocks of our lives, and understanding how they work can empower us to make positive changes. By identifying cues, replacing routines, and rewarding ourselves for the right behaviors, we can shape our habits to align with our goals and aspirations.

Whether you aspire to become more successful in your career or simply want to live a healthier, happier life, harnessing the power of habits is a key step on your journey to personal growth and fulfillment.

And for goodness sake...BE PATIENT! Habits don't form overnight, and they certainly won't change overnight, either. It takes time and consistent effort to rewire your brain. Don't be discouraged by setbacks; they are a natural part of the process. Three steps forward, but two steps back is still progress. Keep focusing on the new routine, and it will eventually become automatic.

There are lots of great books out there on habit building, but here are three of my favs:

- Atomic Habits by James Clear

- The 5 Second Rule by Mel Robbins

- Miracle Morning by Hal Elrod

HABITS SUCCESS STORY:

CARRIE BAKER
58 / Nevada / 16lb weight loss

In the beginning, I was focused on my strength and mobility; however, I wasn't all in. I knew if I didn't do something to change my mindset, I was going to give up. Creating a new habit was my way of controlling my lack of motivation. I made a commitment to myself to work out six days a week before 7:00 am. It was as simple as that! This provided me with structure, motivation, and something to look forward to every day.

3

YOUR ACCOUNTABILITY

This one is HUGE…likely the HUGEST! Not a word, but my word.

Having someone who **NOTICES** and **CARES** when you're not showing up is the critical piece to STAYING ON THE WAGON. We all know WHAT we need to do—eat healthy and move our bodies. So, why aren't we all healthy? We falter with these habits unless we have a strong WHY and a rock-solid **ACCOUNTABILITY PARTNER**.

You're less likely to skip a workout or make that unhealthy food choice if you know someone is paying attention and cares if you don't do the work. Plus, locking arms and doing this healthy lifestyle thing with others makes the experience more enjoyable and social. You will encourage and inspire each other, share your progress, and celebrate victories together.

I know we literally just talked about this in the last chapter, but it's such a critical piece to your success that I MUST dedicate an entire chapter to it! So you'll hear it again here and likely several more times before that last page.

You can have access to the greatest workouts in the world and know exactly which foods are the healthiest to eat; as a matter of fact, you can get all of this free right from Uncle Google. So why, then, aren't you staying consistent with getting your workouts done and making healthy food choices most of the time? Because you don't have ACCOUNTABILITY.

You MUST have someone who NOTICES and CARES when you aren't "showing up" and directly, yet respectfully, taps you on the shoulder to keep you on that wagon.

I was interviewed on a podcast recently and had a respectful disagreement with the host, who said he didn't believe that EVERYONE needed accountability. Oh boy, I couldn't disagree more! I don't care how strong your discipline muscle is; you need someone holding you accountable to your priorities in life. If you don't agree with me, then you, my friend, are a real-life unicorn, and I'd love to touch your perfect arm in hopes your fairy dust rubs off on me.

One VERY IMPORTANT thing to note about your accountability partner…it 100% CANNOT be a significant other or close friend. Their job is to love you just the way you are. And I'm not sure about you, but if my significant other or close friend made a comment about my workouts or nutrition, I just might clock them square between the eyes. Just sayin'.

As you work to interview and find your perfect accountability partner, remember two things:

1. You can "date" initially to test out the relationship. Dating without a full commitment makes it easier to break up if it's not a good fit.

2. You must be prepared to accept direct yet respectful feedback. Cheerleaders feel good, but they won't help you progress if they ONLY tell you how great you are and not call you out on your SHIZ. I will refer you back to the chapter on YOUR MIND to help you with this one.

CREATE YOUR ROADMAP

STEP 1

Find a REAL accountability partner, not a cheerleader or a "yes friend."

STEP 2

Set a trial "dating" period for 30 days.

STEP 3

Repeat steps 1-2 until you find the perfect fit.

BOTTOM LINE:

You MUST have an accountability partner. Someone who NOTICES and CARES when you aren't "showing up" and directly, yet respectfully, taps you on the shoulder to keep you on that wagon. I'm telling you that this has been the key to my consistency and the key for all of my clients who have been consistent with me for years.

ACCOUNTABILITY SUCCESS STORY:

LORI DEUTSCHER
64 / Indiana / 20lb weight loss

Embarking on a health journey following a medical scare feels like uncovering a roadmap to a healthier, more vibrant version of oneself. Five years ago, I faced a pivotal moment, realizing that a sedentary lifestyle with unhealthy snacks wasn't a sustainable choice. I explored various workout programs and diets, but none seemed to resonate. It was akin to searching for a missing puzzle piece in a dark room. Then, I discovered the value of a full wellness system that includes ACCOUNTABILITY. Sharing my daily triumphs and challenges with this supportive community and having an accountability partner who noticed and cared when I wasn't showing up transformed my health journey from a solitary endeavor into a collective adventure. Now, I not only experience physical well-being but also have a group of friends cheering me on – the true champions of my fitness journey!

4

YOUR FOOD

Good nutrition is the cornerstone of a healthy and fulfilling life. It's 80% of us being our healthiest selves. We simply CANNOT out-workout a poor diet…trust me, I've tried. What we eat directly impacts our physical and mental well-being, our energy levels, and our overall quality of life.

I'm not going to dig deep into the science of nutrition with macros, micros, calories, etc. You can get that from a million other health and wellness books. It's all very important, and understanding the general components is critical. However, the wellness industry overcomplicates the science so much that they lose our attention, and some of us even throw our hands up in frustration and quit before we've even gotten started, which makes me incredibly frustrated and sad.

So, you guessed it, what I'm going to focus on with you here is how to take that important science to (A) SIMPLIFY it into real talk and (B) know how to apply it.

One of the most impactful things someone shared with me back in 2008 that has served me so well is this: **We're not ON a diet; we HAVE a diet.** Everything we consume is our diet, both good and bad. Understanding this provides such a relief because thinking you are ON a diet immediately conjures up thoughts of RESTRICTION and DEPRIVATION. And remember that our THOUGHTS control our FEELINGS, which controls our ACTIONS and ultimately affects our RESULTS. So if you stick with me on this, you can relax your shoulders and breathe a sigh of relief because you will NEVER EVER EVER be ON A DIET again! (Sang in my best Taylor Swift voice)

The second most critical piece to your success is to follow a FULL WELLNESS system that isn't just workouts, but one that has a strong focus on nutrition. A nutrition plan that allows for "stupid foods" and LIFE. This is what makes it truly sustainable forever. Outside of a short-term testing period or cleanse/detox, your everyday nutrition plan should NOT contain the word "never." That, my friend, is a restriction plan, another quick fix that promises big results and will likely give you big results that are sadly only temporary and liable to cause you to move even further away from your goals in the long run.

CREATE YOUR ROADMAP

STEP 1.
WATER, WATER, WATER

Oh man, I have no idea how to STRESS the importance of water enough. I could go ALL CAPS or BOLD or use a string of CURSE WORDS, but it still wouldn't be enough! The MOST important component of your nutrition plan is your WATER consumption.

"Water is a miracle hiding in plain sight, a miracle that's not just in your face—it IS your face. And your skin. And your hair, your organs, your muscles (70 percent water), your fat, your bones (22 percent), your marrow, your toenails, and your brain and nervous system. A miracle that's all around us. It IS us." - Darin Olien, Superlife

Adequate hydration is crucial for maintaining optimal bodily functions like transporting nutrients, food digestion, metabolism, temperature regulation, elimination of waste/toxins, joint lubrication, mental clarity, and, you guessed it, weight management. I know, I know, more science that I promised I wouldn't share, but I really need you to understand this water thing!

It's important to note that we experience the same feeling physiologically when we're hungry as we do when we're thirsty. So many times when we think we're hungry, we're usually just thirsty.

Water FAQs & TIPs:

- Drink half of your body weight in ounces per day up to one gallon (Ex. 140 lbs / 2 = 70 ounces of water per day)
- Buy enough water bottles to equal that amount (for example, I have three 25-ounce bottles because I need at least 67 ounces/day)
- Buy water bottles that you LOVE! (i.e., cute, stainless steel, handle, straw, no-spill, fits in purse, etc.)
- Fill them all up before your head hits the pillow each night and set them out so they are ready to go the next day.
- Set milestones to empty them throughout the day (for example, my milestones are 1st bottle empty by noon, 2nd bottle empty by 5 pm, last bottle empty an hour before bed). ALWAYS stop drinking your water an hour before bed, so your sleep isn't interrupted all night long by going to the bathroom.
- If you aren't a huge fan of water, I don't care; drink it anyway! Can you add anything to it? Yes and no. Yes, you can add all-natural things like lemon, limes, cucumbers, etc. to your water for flavor. Yes, you can add the sugar free flavor liquids/packs short term as you work to solidify your water drinking habit. But NO, you cannot continue using the sugar-free flavoring forever. They are loaded with artificial ingredients that are bad for your body and work against you reaching your goals.
- And NO, because I know you're gonna ask…your coffee/tea/shake water DOES NOT count towards your total! We're talking pure, clean, beautiful water!

STEP 2
Test your body

Just because you're eating foods from the HEALTHY FOODS LIST doesn't mean you're eating healthy. It may surprise you to hear this, but not all healthy foods are healthy for everyone's body. Just because a food is on the healthy foods list doesn't mean it's healthy for YOUR body. Our bodies are certainly similar in many ways, but not all ways. So ... if you are feeling frustrated because you feel like you are eating "healthy foods" and working out and still not feeling and looking your best, the likely culprit of that inflammation in your body is probably the wrong healthy foods for YOUR body.

Let me give you an example. I have a digestive disorder called gastroparesis, which means food stays in my stomach for about 45 minutes longer than the average stomach before moving into the small intestine. Therefore, generally, healthy foods like broccoli, cauliflower, and brussel sprouts eaten often or in large portions could send me right to the ER, and they have! They are so high in fiber, which is good for most bodies, but not mine, because that fiber blows up in my stomach and stays there way longer than most, causing extreme pain. So, I eat them in small portions and on occasion because I love them (life in moderation).

So, while I'm not a fan of tracking forever because, yep, say it with me…it's not sustainable for life. No one will or wants to walk around with a little notebook and pencil in their back pocket to write down every morsel they put into their pie hole until the day they die. However, tracking for a month or two initially is important to do this testing and determine which healthy foods—when you eat them—do you operate and feel your best.

What you want to pay attention to is how you feel the DAY OF and the DAY AFTER you eat certain foods, and start keeping a mental note of those foods that don't fare too well for you and your body. Then, if you choose to eat them on occasion for life in moderation, you'll go into it knowing what to expect from that choice.

This is why I take every new client of mine through a 4-week testing program when we first start working together. Having this level of knowledge about your body prevents unnecessary frustration and is a GAME CHANGER!

STEP 3
Plan & Prep

Don't roll your eyes, I saw that. I promise my way is not as painful as you're used to seeing.

Listen, "Meal Prep Sundays" work. However, I would rather take a wooden toothpick and jam it directly into my eyeball than stand in my kitchen for hours on a Sunday to cook and prepare meals. So, how do I create healthy meals and snacks that are easy to GRAB-N-GO without this Sunday madness?

I practice and coach with what I call NOW & LATER. Every time you cook/prepare a meal/snack NOW, simply make extra servings to have LATER. You're already dicing, chopping, and cooking, so making a few extra servings is really not more work. Remember that SIMPLE = SUCCESS. And doesn't this sound so much simpler?

So whether you meal prep on Sundays, if that's your jam, or, like me, you practice NOW & LATER, the end result is the same - you must have healthy "GRAB AND GO."

STEP 4
Ingredient List trumps the Nutrition Label

The nutrition breakdown is certainly important, but you should be WAY MORE focused on the INGREDIENT list than the NUTRITION breakdown.

There's too much focus on calories and not enough on ingredients. Not all calories are created equal, and metabolism is a complicated process. Be more laser-focused on exactly WHAT ingredients you are putting into your body and less on the total calorie count.

For example, the menu at a restaurant shows you that the mushroom ravioli dinner is only 410 calories versus the salmon dinner at 550. The salmon dinner is a much healthier choice because the ingredients are cleaner. The pasta and the cream sauce of the ravioli dinner are loaded with starchy carbs and heavy dairy that wreak havoc on our bodies. So, while it is nice for restaurants to include the calorie count for each dish, it's SUPER MISLEADING and creates confusion for the average consumer.

SUGAR-FREE, CALORIE-FREE, ALL-NATURAL…these are marketing ploys to pull us into thinking that something is healthy. Just because something is sugar-free or calorie-free or all-natural does NOT mean that it's healthy, so turn that sucker over and read that ingredient list. WHAT we eat matters for weight/fat loss and for optimal health!

BOTTOM LINE:

Test your body to determine which of the foods on the healthy food list are healthy for YOUR body; always have healthy GRAB-N-GO ready, nail your water consumption habit, and stop telling me how many calories something has - know the ingredients going into your body.

Let me share this story with you, I think it will help you with your THOUGHTS as it relates to this nutrition piece.

These pictures were taken 11 years apart. NOTE: I am healthy in both pictures.

There's very little difference in what you SEE. However, as I've dialed into what my body NEEDS and WANTS, I've been able to create even more balance than ever before with LIVING LIFE IN MODERATION.

The picture on the left is me at 40 years old, right after a 21-day detox where my nutrition was 100% clean with zero "whites," zero alcohol, and I certainly wasn't eating the f*cking pizza.

The picture on the right is me today at 52 years old, where my nutrition is about 85-90% clean with limited alcohol and eating the f*cking pizza at least once a month.

Today, I eat A LOT more food.

Today, I focus more on ingredients vs total calories.

Today, I am 5 lbs lighter.

Today, and at 40, my body fat is/was 20% (BF is expected to rise as we age).

Today, I eat the f*cking pizza (on occasion).

Have and follow a nutrition plan that is truly sustainable FOR LIFE! Not a restriction plan that will only set you up for failure and a life full of back pocket tracking notebooks.

FOOD SUCCESS STORY:

KIMBERLY DAWN GEDDES
53 / Florida / 50lb weight loss

As a nurse and personal trainer, I thought I had all the answers and had it all figured out, but I found myself getting really frustrated and unhappy with my appearance and the way I was feeling. Sharing my frustration with Mary and considering another "quick fix," she suggested I think long-term and test my body to gain a better understanding of which foods, when I eat them, I feel my best.

WOW…my bloated belly reduced in just the first week, and by the end of the four-week testing period, the inflammation in my entire body was gone! I was already eating really clean, healthy foods, BUT I learned through this testing process that not ALL healthy foods are healthy for MY BODY. I now know which foods when I eat them; I feel my best, so now I can make more informed choices with my food. If I choose to eat foods that aren't "my friend" (crackers are my crack, lol), I know upfront to expect the inflammation to return. But I'll tell ya, while I do live life in moderation, it feels so good to feel this good that I don't choose those foods very often anymore. I feel so good, better than I've felt in a long time!

5

YOUR WORKOUTS

Our workouts are most certainly important, but they are nowhere near as important as our nutrition. And, as you learned so far, none of it trumps the ACCOUNTABILITY piece because we can have a solid workout and nutrition plan, but if we aren't following it, it does us no good.

As I mentioned in my intro of this book, I won't be giving you workouts here or telling you what workout program is best for you. What I will cover are the overarching general principles that have served me so well and my best tips for finding and keeping consistency with the workout piece to your full wellness system because consistency is the key to success in any fitness journey. Whether you're a seasoned athlete or just starting on your path to a healthier lifestyle, maintaining a regular workout routine to move your body is important.

CREATE YOUR ROADMAP

STEP 1.
Plan Your Workout Schedule - Your YOU Time

Consistency often relies on structure. Plan your workouts ahead of time and incorporate them into your daily or weekly schedule. Set specific days and times for exercise, and stick to them unless an emergency arises. Treat your workouts like important appointments that you can't miss, and DO NOT allow people or things to interrupt your workout appointment. I mean this literally: if someone asks if you are available and it's during your workout appointment, your answer is, "No, however, here's a day/time that works better for me." The more you integrate your workouts into your routine, the less likely you are to skip them.

One of the most common questions I get is, "What is the best time to workout?" The best time to workout is the time when you'll get the workout done. HOWEVER, that being said, getting your workout done first thing in the morning is best for many reasons: (A) It's less likely to get interrupted by someone or something, (B) it is physiologically best for your body as it will burn reserved fats and calories, (C) it gives you energy for your long day ahead and (D) likely the most valuable reason—it is a fabulous mindset winner—aligning your THOUGHTS in a positive, sense-of-accomplishment space.

STEP 2.
Find Workouts You ENJOY!

One of the most effective ways to stay consistent with working out is to choose workouts you genuinely enjoy. You know what they say? The best workout is the one you'll actually do! There is so much out there now, so explore various forms of exercise like weight training, boxing, dancing, yoga, Pilates, barre, cycling, swimming, hiking, etc. until you find ones that excite you. I despise "plugged-in equipment" (aka treadmill, elliptical, etc)…boring! Cardio (aka cardiovascular conditioning) is nothing more than elevating your heart rate. You can have way more fun doing that through short 20-40 minute EFFICIENT and EFFECTIVE weight lifting or HIIT (High-Intensity Interval Training) type workouts. When you look forward to your workouts, you'll be more likely to stick with them. So, find workouts you love; they do exist!

STEP 3.
Spice It Up

Variety is the spice of life, and it's also essential for maintaining consistency in your workouts. Doing the same workout day after day can lead to boredom and burnout. To keep things fresh and exciting mentally and physically, mix up your workouts by incorporating different types of workouts like we talked about above. It will make working out more fun and help you avoid the dreaded plateau.

STEP 4.
Set Short-Term Milestones

In addition to your long-term fitness goals, establish short-term milestones. These can be weekly or monthly targets that lead you toward your larger objectives. Short-term goals give you a sense of achievement and help you stay motivated. For example, if your long-term goal is to run a marathon, a short-term milestone could be running 4 miles without stopping in month one. Or if your long-term goal is to lose 100 pounds, a short-term milestone could be to lose the first 10 pounds in month one.

STEP 5.
Track Your Progress

Monitoring your progress is a powerful motivator. Keep a workout journal or use fitness apps and wearable devices to record your achievements. Documenting your workouts, tracking your weight, and measuring your body composition allows you to see how far you've come and reminds you of your dedication.

BE SURE NOT to measure progress on the scale alone! The scale is not the enemy, but it's only ONE measure of progress. For example, if your goal is to lose weight, then your goal is to be a smaller human, correct? If you only measure your progress with the scale and the scale either goes up or doesn't move, you'll likely think you haven't made progress. HOWEVER, if you weigh yourself AND take body composition measurements and you've lost inches, then you are most certainly becoming a smaller human, correct? See why it's important to do both? And remember that building muscle can also cause the scale to fluctuate.

Celebrate your successes, no matter how small they may seem. Note: avoid celebrating with food; choose some fun, new workout clothes instead.

One more important note about the scale. Unless you have a very serious, unhealthy relationship with the scale, you should weigh yourself EVERY SINGLE DAY. Not once a week or once a month. WHY? Because you could be having a great week—getting your workouts done, eating healthy, drinking your water, etc. Then, Friday after work, you go out to celebrate a friend's birthday or something, and "life in moderation," you have a drink or a meal that isn't the healthiest. Well, if Saturday morning is "weigh day," then that scale is likely to move in the wrong direction, WHICH will cause you to think you had a bad week. When, in fact, you had a great week and are probably just retaining water from the cocktail or "stupid foods" from the prior day. The scale is usually a direct reflection of the prior day, not the entire week. So, weigh daily and monitor your weekly averages to truly track your scale progress.

STEP 6.
Don't Overtrain

More does not always equal better, especially when it comes to your workouts. Don't get hung up or waste time worrying about calories burned. Most monitors are inaccurate by 30-50%. Trust your workout program and just move your body.

Overtraining and burnout can hinder your consistency. Make sure to incorporate adequate rest days and recovery time into your routine. This includes getting enough sleep, allowing time for muscle repair, and listening to your body when it needs a break. Recovery is a crucial part of long-term consistency and overall fitness success.

STEP 7.
Give Yourself Some Grace

Life is full of unexpected twists and turns. There will be days when you can't stick to your planned workout schedule due to work commitments, family obligations, illness, or unexpected events. In such cases, be flexible, adapt, and give yourself some grace. Find alternative ways to stay active that day, possibly by doing a shorter workout or simply switching up rest days that week.

And don't forget MARY'S 3-DAY RULE: Never hit day 3 of poor choices. Miss a workout or two, no worries, no guilt, but NEVER miss 3 in a row!

STEP 8.
Cute Workout Clothes

For the love of all things Holy, stop working out in old, ratty t-shirts and sweats. Buy yourself some cute workout clothes! They don't have to be expensive but feel good in what you're wearing for your workouts. YES, it matters, even if you are working out all alone at home. It affects your THOUGHTS, which affects your FEELINGS, which affects your ACTIONS, and ultimately affects your RESULTS. It may seem silly to some, but it's more motivating and powerful than you may think. Test it and see.

Oh, and while we're on the subject of workout clothes…lay your workout clothes out before your head hits the pillow each night. It's one less decision and thing you have to do at 0:DARK:30.

STEP 9.
Gym vs Home Workouts

The best place to workout is the place where you'll get the workout done! I spent years arguing with myself that I had to go to the gym to get the best workouts. However, in 2008, after being sick and tired of NOT getting it done, I was open to change. And I'm so grateful I was because it has completely changed my life! You wouldn't be reading this book right now if I hadn't made that change.

There is absolutely NOTHING wrong with gyms…as long as you go. It's the GO part that trips many of you up. If you are finding that you aren't making it happen with your gym workouts, then I may suggest you be open to change like I was and give home-based workouts a try.

Here are some of the advantages of a home-based system that I've personally experienced:
- saves money
- saves time
- no waiting on equipment
- equipment is clean
- no gawking people
- no witnesses for incontinence challenges (IYKYK ladies)

If you do elect to give home-based workouts a go, don't overwhelm yourself by thinking you have to purchase thousands of dollars worth of equipment. A set of light, medium, and heavy dumbbells is a perfect start. You can slowly build your home gym over time as you progress in your workouts.

STEP 10.
Stay Positive and Stay Patient

Consistency in working out is a journey, not a destination. There will be setbacks and plateaus along the way, but it's essential to stay positive and patient. Celebrate your successes, no matter how small, and don't be too hard on yourself when you face challenges. Remember that building a strong, healthy body is a lifelong endeavor, and each workout is a step in the right direction.

BOTTOM LINE:

Staying consistent with working out is the foundation of achieving your fitness goals. By setting clear goals, creating a schedule, enjoying your workouts, and implementing these tips, you can establish a lasting commitment to your health and well-being. Remember that consistency is not about perfection but about making progress one step at a time. Stay motivated, stay consistent, and watch as your fitness journey transforms your life.

WORKOUT SUCCESS STORY:

TINA ASHLEY
51 / Georgia / 10lb weight loss

Mid-life crept up on me unexpectedly, its subtle changes compounding over time. Faced with unexplained symptoms, I navigated through the challenges, searching for a solution. For three decades prior to the mid-life challenges, I had battled trying to lose 20-40 pounds struggling to find a sustainable routine, but everything seemed even more difficult in this new stage of life. Then, I found a full wellness program that proved to be a game-changer! Not only shifting my mindset and fostering consistency, but I unexpectedly FELL IN LOVE WITH EXERCISE, which was transforming not just my body but my entire approach to health.

So, what was different about my new workouts? They were convenient (home-based), giving me flexibility and saving me time and money. They also offered a vast array of different types of workouts and trainer styles, and that variety proved powerful for both my mind and my body.

It feels great to have finally found something that works for me and will be my forever fitness lifestyle. I am grateful that I didn't give up on myself and that I was willing to try something new. That "something new" was just the thing I had been looking for!

6

YOUR MODERATION

Unless you've skipped to the back of the book and/or didn't understand the powerful message behind this book's title, by now, you should have picked up on the two main themes - **KEEP IT SIMPLE** and **LIFE IN MODERATION**.

These two critical pieces are what will guarantee you a healthy lifestyle that is truly SUSTAINABLE FOR LIFE!

These two critical pieces are what the health and wellness industry fails to help us with.

These two critical pieces are what prevent so many of us from starting.

These two critical pieces are what prevent so many of us from figuring it out sooner.

These two critical pieces are what prevent so many of us from staying on the wagon.

We touched on life in moderation in every chapter, but I felt it was super important to end with it so you really get the message LOUD AND CLEAR!

This healthy lifestyle thing is a journey, my friend, a marathon, not a sprint. Think of it like a staircase; take it one step at a time to KEEP IT SIMPLE and to AVOID OVERWHELM. Remember that overwhelm is a choice. No one or nothing can overwhelm you. You overwhelm yourself.

CREATE YOUR ROADMAP

STEP 1

Moderation means we aren't striving for perfection. Perfection is neither achievable nor sustainable.

STEP 2

Moderation means we don't have to workout for hours and hours 7 days a week to be healthy.

STEP 3

Moderation means we don't have to eat 100% clean, healthy foods 7 days a week to be healthy.

STEP 4

Moderation means we don't have to be alcohol-free unless we choose to be or we have a condition that requires it.

STEP 5

Moderation means we don't have to skip the cake at a birthday party. Are you kidding me right now?! I will b*tch slap you right through this book if you don't EAT THE F*CKING PIECE OF CAKE! Just don't eat the whole cake, k?

STEP 6

Moderation means we enjoy food. Food is NOT the enemy. Food is amazing and to be enjoyed and celebrated. We just want to strive to have a healthy relationship with food, as discussed in the YOUR FOOD chapter.

BOTTOM LINE:

Moderation means we EAT THE F*CKING PIZZA! Just not every day!

MODERATION SUCCESS STORY:

RITA LINN

49 / South Dakota / 17lb weight loss and maintaining now at desired weight

"Oh my gosh, if I EVER have to diet and exercise to lose weight and be healthy, I'll just roll over and die!" That's what I told myself every time I watched someone bounce from one trendy "diet" to the next. So many rules and restrictions and some downright crazy concepts. Well, fast forward a couple of decades and jeans sizes later, and guess who was feeling like crap and needing to go on a "diet?"

I hit my 40s, and my life turned upside down - I bought my dream horse ranch, got married, became a stepmom, and lost both of my parents. I was busier and more active than ever, yet I still packed on an extra 15-ish lbs. (that's a lot for a small 5'5" frame). I didn't feel my best, and I definitely didn't feel strong enough to live out my dream on the ranch.

How was I going to find the time to feel better, exercise every day and eat healthy, especially with picky eaters in the house? That's when I found a full wellness system designed for REAL LIFE. I learned that I didn't have to do those things 100% perfect EVERY day. I learned what could be done to get real results while still living a "normal" life and not going crazy in the process. I learned what my body liked and didn't like so that it operates at its best.

I eat amazing, easy-to-prepare healthy food with my picky family, workout only 4 days a week, and still eat Deb's famous broasted chicken with fries and a Bloody Mary on occasion! I lost 21 lbs, 16 inches, and 2 jean sizes, living healthy in moderation. I'm stronger than I've ever been, have more energy, and feel great! Small changes at a time can lead to big results without totally depriving yourself of the things you love. If I can do this, you can too!!

7

YOUR KICKASS NEW LIFE!

Well, there you go, the super easy secret sauce to being your healthiest self and living your best life! Uh, negative ghostrider!

Expect to fail MANY TIMES! But learn how to embrace failures and FAIL FORWARD. The most successful people in this world failed countless times before the success that we know them for.

Getting back up, dusting yourself off, and continuing on your journey is what will separate YOU as a WINNER from the LOSERS.

You are not allowed to throw your hands up and quit. I will come after you.

You heard my story; I spent most of my adult life trying and failing on that maddening yo-yo rollercoaster ride. BUT the reason this book even exists and is in your hands is that I **FAILED FORWARD**.

We have two choices when we fall off that wagon…AGAIN:

1. Sulk, blame others for our failure, claim it's not obtainable, and quit.

OR

2. Get pissed and let it fuel us to refocus, reassess and TRY AGAIN!

I'll take door #2, please, Monty.

Life is FULL of FAILURES, so why would we think experiencing them makes US a failure??

Progress always beats perfection.

> Let's FAIL FORWARD, my friend. It serves us better and puts us in a very exclusive league with some of THE GREATS out there.

> Let's also take a hot minute to CELEBRATE THE $H!T out of all the WINS! Don't tell me there were none; I'll find them for you if you can't see them.

It doesn't matter how old or young we are; we have everything we need to do the work to create the life, the friendships, and the daily habits that we choose for our lives.

Stop waiting for other people to do it for you. Wake up every day and choose to make it your best.

Yes, I'm talking to YOU. Whatever it is that you want to achieve in life…make it happen!

Stop wishin' and bitchin'…make TODAY the day where you draw a line in the sand and reinvent yourself. You can reinvent yourself whenever you want.

"Your age isn't stopping you from living your best life, your excuses are."

- Mel Robbins

I BELIEVE IN YOU! Now, go create the life you want because I need you here with me! I want your life to be as happy, healthy, and fulfilling as mine so we can lock arms and rock this life together with Rockin' Vitality!

Let's make the **LAST HALF** the **BEST HALF** rockstar!

BOTTOM LINE:

Get healthy between the ears with daily **MIND**set work. Understand WHY you want to reach your goals to help you draw on your internal motivation to get your shiz done.

Build your healthy **HABITS**, your new normal, one step at a time through your habit loop.

Find an honest and loving **ACCOUNTABILITY** partner who notices and cares when you aren't showing up and respectfully calls you out!

Follow a **FOOD** plan that allows for "stupid foods" on occasion so it is truly sustainable for life!

Find **WORKOUTS** that are efficient, effective, and enjoyable!

Embrace **MODERATION** in every single aspect of your wellness plan!

Enjoy your **KICKASS NEW LIFE** and make your last half your best half!

KICKASS LIFE SUCCESS STORY:

MIKE O'CALLAHAN
52 / Illinois / 50lb weight loss

I became consistent with an at-home workout program on DVDs, but how did I stay on track during the week when I traveled? I did what I had to do because it was a priority for me - "where there is a will, there is a way." I bought a portable DVD player and brought the DVDs with me (no more DVDs now with streaming services). I chose the "no equipment required" workouts, so I could easily do them from anywhere (hotel room, hotel gym, even Bora Bora!). I just needed the time and the will to do them. Consistency creates a routine, so I remain disciplined and committed no matter where I travel. And hey, not only do I want to look good, I want to FEEL good too. That's what keeps me on track.

ACKNOWLEDGEMENTS

To MY ROCKSTARS, MY INFLUENCERS:

Mary's Crüe, the ultimate focus group.

Regina Lively, the killer cover design.

Celia Bloom, Regina Lively & Rita Linn, the best Beta Readers eva.

Regina Lively, Carrie Baker, Tina Ashley, Kimberly Dawn Geddes, Rita Linn, Lori Deutscher and Mike O'Callahan the most inspiring success storytellers.

Nicholas Carter, the editor I never knew I needed.

Katalin Fodor, the kickass cover photographer.

LeeAnn Gordon for introducing me to a better way.

Scott Ingrassia for introducing me to a way to pay it forward to help you.

Heather Johnson, the success partner who held me accountable to write the f*cking book!

Amanda, the most rockstar assistant who quite literally gave me my life back.

Demetrios Pizza for the mouthwatering pizza on my photoshoot!

And my Paul, who has NEVER wavered in his belief in me!

ADDITIONAL RESOURCES

THE THOUGHT MODEL

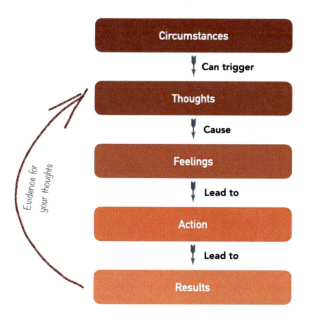

The Model: A simple tool to create awareness around your thoughts and shift your thinking so you can create new results. It is made up of five interrelated parts: circumstance, thought, feeling, action, and result.

C = Circumstance: Circumstances are the neutral facts of the situation. Examples include the time, the place, the exact words someone says, exact numbers that are factual. They are written without adjectives or judgment, as neutral as possible. Ex: I haven't lost weight.

T = Thought: Thoughts are triggered by a circumstance. Also known as the story, it is how your brain interprets the circumstance. For example, what did you think or make it mean when you got on the scale and saw you hadn't lost weight? You will notice lots of thoughts in your brain dump. Simply select one to put to use in your self-coaching.

F = Feeling: A feeling is a vibration in your body that is fueled by a thought. For example, you may feel overwhelmed, anxious, inadequate, or defeated. You might notice several emotions at once. If this happens, choose one feeling at a time to work on.

A = Action: Actions are what you do or don't do in response to how you feel. Notice that your actions don't just happen. They're always connected to your thoughts and feelings. Examples of actions include hiding, asking for help, comparing, judging, complaining, numbing/buffering, working, quitting, scrolling social, etc.

R = Result: This is the effect of your Action line. It is also what your brain learns from your thoughts, feelings, and actions. The Result always reinforces what you think.

Rockin' Vitality Retreat

Rockin' Vitality Retreat is my annual wellness retreat. The perfect fusion of WELLNESS and 80s ROCK. Guaranteed to be the MOST KICKASS FUN you've ever had at a HEALTH RETREAT!

Spend 3 days with me and other like-minded, healthy-striving, fun people learning how to live your HAPPIEST, HEALTHIEST, and BEST LIFE while reliving the best music ever created—our beloved 80s Rock!

My mission is to help you find your JOY again, your ENERGY again, your ZEST FOR LIFE again ... help you feel MORE ALIVE than you may have ever felt before!

Grab the deets here: https://view.flodesk.com/pages/64d67c4778891ef5c9a2f455

ABOUT THE AUTHOR

Mary is a former Corporate Healthcare Executive and Chronic Yo-Yo Dieter turned Health & Wellness Coach and Entrepreneur, helping people simplify, achieve and sustain healthy habits to stay 'ON THE WAGON' of healthy living forever.

Mary spent over 23 years as a Healthcare Executive, most of those years taking care of our greatest generation as a Nursing Home Administrator.

In 2012, she began her entrepreneurial journey as CEO and Founder of Team Faithfully Fit. Helping customers to stop the crazy yo-yo dieting madness by creating consistency in healthy habits that are rooted in faith and positivity and truly sustainable for life.

Mary enjoys her free time with husband Paul, son Jake, grandson Forest… Oh, and her beautiful Golden Retrievers, Max and Willow.

Mary believes strongly that it is God's divine PURPOSE and CALLING for her life to serve His Kingdom by coaching His children to consistently operate from their place of greatness!

WHERE TO FIND ME

IG: https://www.instagram.com/mary.schrank/

TT: https://www.tiktok.com/@maryschrank

FB: https://www.facebook.com/CoachMaryBiz/

My Kickass Playlist: https://music.apple.com/us/playlist/faithfully-fit-warrior/pl.u-vxy6kLDFPPoxyx

Made in the USA
Middletown, DE
18 May 2025

75703601R00024